WITHDRAWN

LIGHT FRUIT DESSERTS

IMP Limited

CONTENTS

POPULAR EXOTIC FRUIT

The wide range of tropical fruit available in supermarkets provides ample scope for creating exotic desserts. Here's how to buy, store and prepare the most popular ones.

Fruit	Peak Season	Buying & Storing	Preparation
Lychee	Available all year round (imported from China, South Africa, Taiwan, Thailand, India, Australia)	Buy firm fruit with unbroken skin and a pink tinge. Keep in the fridge for up to 2 weeks.	**1** Break open the brittle skin with your fingernail or a sharp knife. Pop out the fruit.
Kiwi Fruit	Available all year round (imported June – Jan from New Zealand; Nov – May from Italy)	Ripe fruit will 'give' to the touch; firm fruit will ripen at room temperature. Store ripe fruit in fridge for 5 days.	**1** Peel the fruit, removing just the skin and as little flesh as possible.
Mango	Available all year round (imported from Brazil, Pakistan, Venezuela, Jamaica, India)	Ripe fruit gives to the touch and smells fragrant. Store firm fruit for 3 weeks in fridge or 10 days at room temperature.	**1** Cut down either side of the stone, taking off as much flesh as possible.
Papaya (Pawpaw)	Available all year round (imported from Jamaica, Brazil, South Africa, Malaysia, Israel)	Buy ripe fruit (just soft to the touch) with no soft patches; it can be green to orange. Store for 5 days at room temperature.	**1** Cut in half lengthways and scoop out the black seeds with a spoon.
Pineapple	Available all year round (imported from Costa Rica, Ghana, Hawaii, Ivory Coast)	Buy ripe fruit (with a sweet smell and top leaves easy to pull off). Store in fridge for 3–4 days.	**1** Slice off the base so the fruit will stand upright, then cut the skin off in long downward strips.

2 Cut round the flesh, peel it back, then lift out the stone.

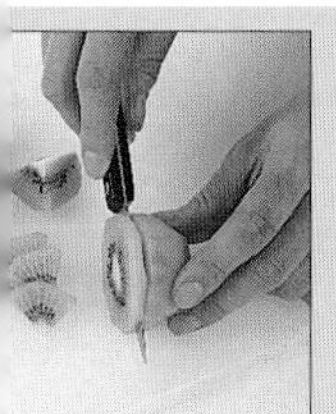

2 Cut off the hard stem end and halve, slice or quarter the flesh.

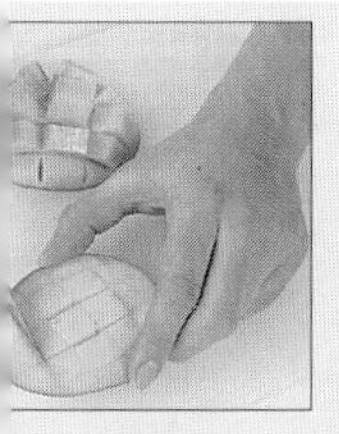

2 Make criss-cross cuts in each section, and push from skin side to 'hedgehog' the flesh.

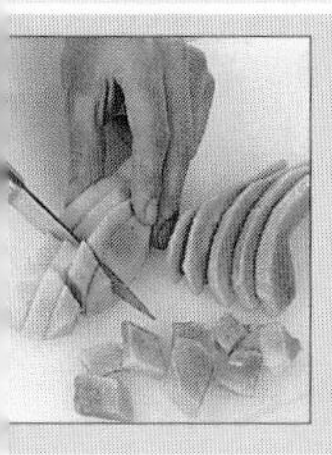

2 Pare off the thin skin and slice or dice the flesh.

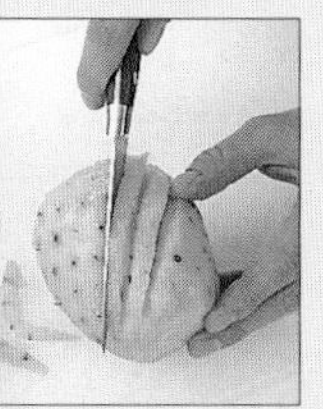

2 Cut out the fibrous 'eyes' in diagonal strips. Halve, cut out the hard core; slice or chop the flesh.

Decorating with Fruit

For apple fruit fans, quarter the apple and trim off the core. Cut wedges of decreasing size and pull apart.

For strawberry fruit fans, slice each berry several times without cutting through the stalk end; press gently to open out. Arrange them on serving plates or dishes as a decoration with your favourite desserts.

For fruit peel flowers, pare long strips of rind from citrus fruits with a sharp knife or canelle knife. Trim off any white pith. Curl the pieces of rind round to form a spiral. Use to decorate citrus-flavoured puddings and desserts.

For chocolate-dipped fruits, such as grapes and strawberries. Melt some milk, plain or white chocolate. Half-dip the fruits into the chocolate, then leave to set on a sheet of foil. Great served with ice cream or fruit mousse or as an after-dinner nibble.

To frost small bunches of redcurrants, dip small sprigs in lightly whisked egg white, then dip in caster sugar. Leave to dry on a wire rack. Use to decorate cakes, soufflés and mousses.

For lychee flowers, score through the skin towards the stalk at regular intervals, using a small, sharp knife. Carefully peel back and open out the skin to form a flower.

*C*ARIBBEAN ORANGE CUPS

BAHAMAS

The contrast of tart fruit, such as grapefruit and redcurrants, served with a sweet coconut and lime sauce makes a refreshing dessert. Orange shells make attractive serving containers.

INGREDIENTS
(Serves 4)

- 2 large oranges
- 1 kiwi fruit
- 1 pink grapefruit
- 1 lime
- 3 tbsp caster sugar
- 4 tbsp coconut liqueur
- 50g/2oz redcurrants
- 1 small banana

INGREDIENTS TIP

If you don't have any coconut liqueur, mix equal quantities of white rum and an exotic fruit juice, such as pineapple. Many off licences sell miniature bottles of liqueur, which avoids the necessity of buying a whole bottle when only a little is needed for a recipe. If you want to drop the alcohol altogether, replace the coconut liqueur with your favourite fruit juice.

1 Wash the oranges in hot water and dry. Working over a chopping board to catch the juice, cut each orange in half through the centre. Cut around the flesh inside the peel with a knife, keeping the skin intact. Lift out the segments and remove their membranes. With a sharp knife, remove the pith from the orange shell.

Step 1

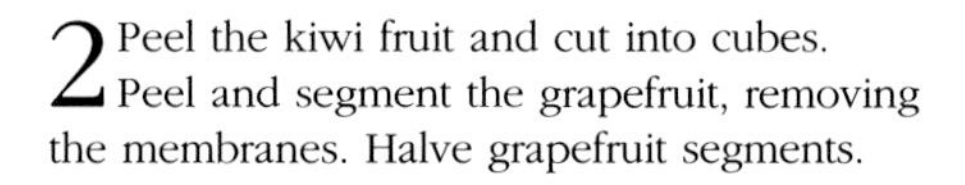

2 Peel the kiwi fruit and cut into cubes. Peel and segment the grapefruit, removing the membranes. Halve grapefruit segments.

Step 2

3 Wash the lime in hot water and pat dry; grate the rind and squeeze the juice. Put both into a bowl and mix with the sugar, coconut liqueur and any orange or grapefruit juices saved when preparing the fruits.

4 Wash the redcurrants and pull from their stalks by sliding each sprig between the prongs of a fork. Peel the banana and cut into 6mm/¼in thick slices.

5 Mix the orange segments, kiwi fruit and grapefruit with the banana and redcurrants and toss gently together. Spoon into the halved orange shells and pour over the lime juice mixture. Serve immediately.

Step 5

Preparation **35** Min
Per Serving: 169 kcal/716 kJ;
2g protein; 0.4g fat;
33g carbohydrate

TYPICALLY CARIBBEAN

The hot Caribbean climate is ideal for growing exotic fruits and vegetables such as mangoes, plantain and okra. Caribbean food is often hot and spicy – an influence introduced by West African slaves – and fruit is often mixed with spicy ingredients in the same savoury dish.

Cooking Tips

If you are preparing the fruit a little while before eating, toss the banana pieces in the lime juice mixture to prevent them from discolouring. Keep the fruit separate and assemble at the last minute • After you have hollowed out the orange halves, cut a thin slice from the bottom to make them stand steady.

Serving Tip

Crunchy pieces of fresh coconut are delicious with this salad. Crack the coconut and, using a small, sharp knife, cut the flesh away from the shell and into small, wedge-shaped pieces.

SERVING TIP Lightly toasting the flakes of fresh coconut gives them a delicious flavour and crisp texture. Serve with a shot of white rum, or with a glass of still or sparkling mineral water.

CREOLE FRUIT SALAD

BARBADOS

Exotic fruit from the Caribbean islands sprinkled with grated coconut and served with a delicious banana 'sauce' makes a light dessert that adds a tropical finale to any meal.

INGREDIENTS

(Serves 4)

- 1 small coconut
- 1 mango
- 1 orange
- 2 figs
- 1 guava
- 1 banana
- 1 tbsp caster sugar
- 1 tbsp lemon juice
- 2-3 tbsp white rum

INGREDIENTS TIP

Eat guavas as soon as their green skin turns yellow, indicating ripeness. They should also give slightly when pressed. Aromatic with a sweet but acidic taste, guavas are packed with vitamin C - up to 10 times the amount in citrus fruits. If fresh guavas are unavailable, use drained canned guava halves. Substitute the rum with mango juice, if wished.

1 To extract the coconut milk, stand the coconut on a crumpled tea towel and pierce two holes in the shell using a hammer and a metal skewer. Pour out the milk. Crack the shell with the hammer, prise out the flesh with a knife and rinse clean.

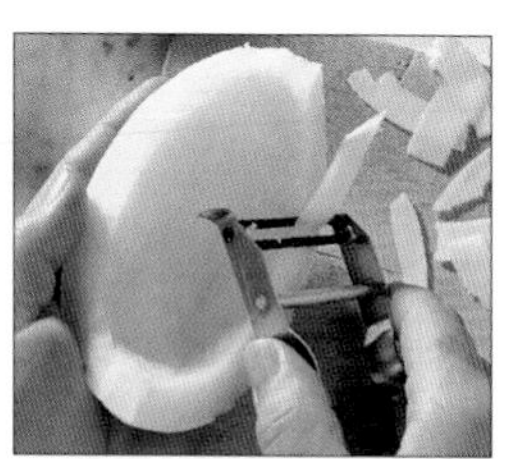

Step 2

2 Shave half of the coconut flesh into flakes with a wide-bladed vegetable peeler and set aside. Grate the rest into a small bowl and cover with 90ml/3fl oz boiling water. Leave to soak for 15 minutes.

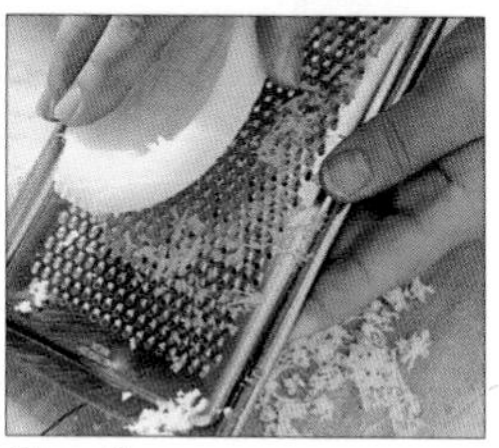

Step 2

3 Peel the mango. Cut the flesh from the stone and cut each piece into slices. Peel and segment the orange, removing all the membrane. Rinse, dry and quarter the figs. Peel the guava and cut into fine slices.

4 Put the soaked coconut into a tea towel and squeeze it over a plate to extract the milk. Peel the banana and purée in a food processor or blender with the sugar, lemon juice and coconut milk.

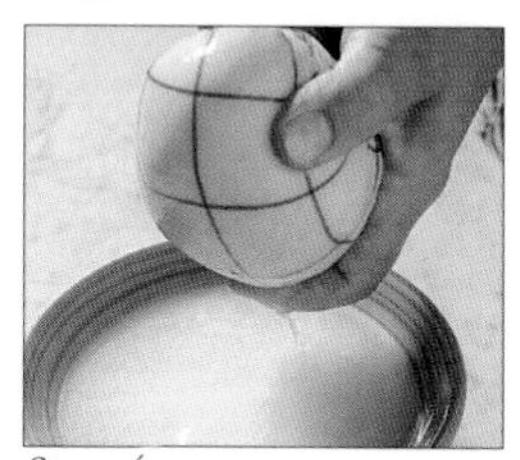

Step 4

5 Divide the grated coconut between four plates. Spoon over the banana 'sauce' and arrange the fruit on top. Pour over the rum and sprinkle with the coconut flakes.

Preparation **20** Min
Per Serving: 194 kcal/811 kJ;
2g protein; 9g fat; 22g carbohydrate

TYPICALLY BARBADIAN

While some of the architecture on Barbados reflects the influence of British colonial rule (1628-1966), the Caribbean islands have a unique cuisine. Known as 'Creole', it is characterized by spiced and curried mixtures of meats, fish and vegetables, served with rice.

BANANAS WITH CARAMELIZED PINEAPPLE

MEXICO

INGREDIENTS
(Serves 4)

- 1 small pineapple
- 60g/2½oz butter
- 3 tbsp brown sugar
- 75ml/2½fl oz tequila or rum
- 4 small bananas
- 3 tbsp lemon juice

TO DECORATE
- 40g/1½oz plain chocolate

INGREDIENTS TIP

Although pineapple has a tough skin, it is delicate. The flavour is spoiled by cold and the flesh bruises easily if the fruit is squeezed too hard. Ripe pineapple smells sweet and fragrant and resists pressure when squeezed; also the small leaves at the crown centre pull off easily. Use pineapple juice instead of tequila or rum, if preferred.

These bananas are covered with hot pineapple cubes laced with the great Mexican spirit, tequila, and sprinkled with smooth, dark chocolate flakes. Sensational!

1 Put the chocolate in the freezer while you prepare the fruit. Slice off the pineapple's leafy top and remove the skin by cutting it off in slices down the length of the fruit. Cut out any dark eyes that remain in the flesh.

Step 1

2 Quarter the pineapple lengthways, cut out and discard the tough core from the centre of each quarter. Cut the flesh into slices and then into bite-sized pieces.

3 Melt the butter in a frying pan over a low heat. Add the sugar and stir constantly until it has dissolved.

Step 3

4 Turn up the heat, add the pineapple cubes and sauté for 5 minutes, stirring constantly. Take off the heat and stir in the tequila, rum or pineapple juice.

5 Peel the bananas and cut in half lengthways. Put two halves on each plate and drizzle with lemon juice. Pour the sauce, with the pineapple cubes, over the bananas.

6 Take the chocolate out of the freezer and shave off small chocolate flakes with a wide-bladed vegetable peeler. Sprinkle over the fruit. Serve immediately.

Step 6

Preparation **20** Min
Per Serving: 402 kcal/1684 kJ;
2g protein; 16g fat; 56g carbohydrate

TYPICALLY MEXICAN

Mexico's national drink, tequila, is a strong-tasting spirit that is fermented from the sap of a cactus-like plant *Agave tequilana*. By law the plants must be grown in the states of Jalisco, Michoacán or Nayarit for the tequila made from them to be genuine.

Cooking tip

Make sure you do not overheat the butter as it will burn quickly. Keep the heat low, add the sugar to the pan as soon as the butter has melted and stir until the sugar dissolves. If the sugar boils before it melts, the sauce will have a crunchy texture rather than being a smooth syrupy mixture.

Serving tip

To go with the Mexican dessert, try a Margarita – a tequila-based cocktail. For each person mix crushed ice with 3 tbsp tequila, 2 tbsp fresh lime juice and 1 tbsp orange liqueur in a shaker or jug. Shake or stir and serve.

Caribbean Mango and Coconut Mousse

Jamaica

This delicate dessert is full of Caribbean flavours. Coconut, puréed mango and rum are whipped into a light mousse and complemented by succulent slices of fresh mango.

INGREDIENTS
(Serves 4)

- 2 sachets gelatine powder
- 100g/4oz creamed coconut
- 450ml/¾ pint milk
- 3 tbsp white rum or mango juice
- 1 lime
- ¼ tsp vanilla essence
- 60g/2½oz caster sugar
- pinch of salt
- 3 ripe mangoes

TO GARNISH

- 1 tbsp cocoa powder
- mint sprigs

Ingredients Tip

If you prefer, you can use a vegetarian powdered setting agent (several brands are available from large supermarkets). Always check the packet before using as quantities needed and instructions can differ from ordinary gelatine.

1 Put 125ml/4fl oz water in a small bowl and sprinkle over the gelatine. Dissolve by standing the bowl in a pan of simmering water for 5 minutes. Remove from the heat.

2 Cut the creamed coconut into squares and put into a pan with the milk. Melt the coconut over a gentle heat, stirring frequently. Remove from the heat; stir in the dissolved gelatine. Grate the rind from the lime and squeeze the juice.

Step 2

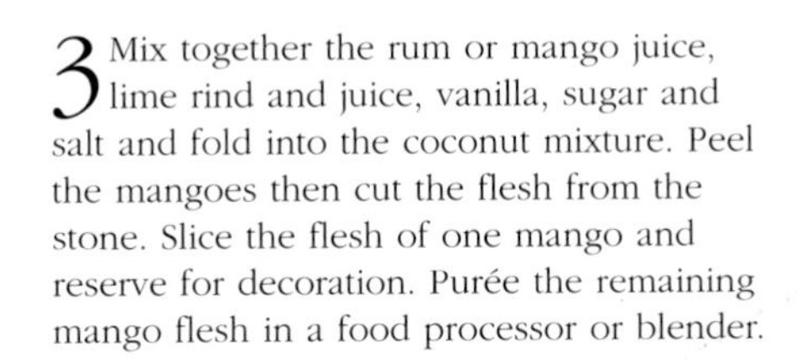

3 Mix together the rum or mango juice, lime rind and juice, vanilla, sugar and salt and fold into the coconut mixture. Peel the mangoes then cut the flesh from the stone. Slice the flesh of one mango and reserve for decoration. Purée the remaining mango flesh in a food processor or blender.

Step 3

4 Stir the puréed mango into the coconut and rum mixture. Put in the fridge for about 3 hours, or until the mixture is set.

Step 3

5 Put the cocoa powder in a fine sieve and shake over the rims of four serving plates. Divide the mango slices between the plates and add scoops of the mango mousse. Decorate each serving with a sprig of mint.

Preparation **30** Min
Chilling **3** Hours
Per Serving: 602 kcal/2493 kJ;
7g protein; 53g fat; 22g carbohydrate

Typically Jamaican

Sugar cane grows all over Jamaica and many other West Indian islands, making sugar one of the islands' main exports. The cane is also used to make the famous Caribbean rum. Most islands make their own variety, the colour of which varies from brownish-red to white.

Cooking tip

If you prefer, replace the milk and creamed coconut in the ingredients with home-made coconut milk. Pour 200ml/7fl oz hot water over 200g/7oz desiccated coconut in a bowl. Leave the mixture to stand for 20 minutes, then drain the milk through a clean cloth into another bowl.

Serving tip

Serve with a piña colada. For one, blend 125ml/4fl oz pineapple juice, 50g/2oz coconut cream, 3 tbsp golden rum and 125ml/4fl oz crushed ice in a blender and pour into a glass.

TEXAN GOLDEN FRUIT COBBLER

USA

Juicy peach slices and sweet blueberries hide under a golden sponge in this traditional American summer fruit bake. Serve straight from the oven, with scoops of vanilla ice cream.

INGREDIENTS

(Serves 4)

- 75g/3oz soft butter, plus extra for greasing
- 2 ripe peaches
- 100g/4oz blueberries
- 75g/3oz caster sugar
- 1 small egg
- 75g/3oz plain flour
- 1 tsp baking powder
- ¼ tsp ground cinnamon
- 5 tbsp milk

TO SERVE

- 4 scoops vanilla ice cream
- 4 mint sprigs

INGREDIENTS TIP

If preferred, you can use frozen blueberries, which are available all year round in most large supermarkets. In autumn, try substituting cooking apples for peaches.

1 Preheat the oven to 180°C/350°F/Gas 4. Lightly butter four small ovenproof dishes, each with a capacity of about 300ml/½ pint. Wash and quarter the peaches, discarding the stones. Cut lengthways into thin slices.

Step 1

2 Carefully rinse the blueberries in a sieve under cold water and drain. Divide the blueberries and peach slices between the dishes, spreading them in an even layer.

3 To make the sponge topping, put the butter and caster sugar in a bowl and beat until pale and creamy. Add the egg and beat again until it is evenly incorporated.

Step 3

4 Sift the flour, baking powder and ground cinnamon into the bowl. Stir with a large spoon to blend all the ingredients together. Gradually stir in the milk. Divide the sponge mixture between the four dishes and spread out to cover the fruit.

Step 4

5 Bake in the oven for 30 minutes, or until the topping is golden brown and firm to the touch. Add a scoop of vanilla ice cream to each dish, decorate with a mint sprig and serve before the ice cream melts.

Preparation **20** Min Cooking **30** Min
Per Serving: 355 kcal/1490 kJ;
5g protein; 18g fat; 45g carbohydrate

TYPICALLY TEXAN

Succulent, golden peaches and sweet, dark-skinned blueberries grow in abundance in Texas. The fertile area around the mouth of the Colorado river in the south eastern corner of the state is particularly good for fruit and vegetable farming due to its sunny climate.

Cooking tip

You can peel the peaches for the cobbler if you prefer. Ideally the peaches need to be ripe but not too soft. Put them into a bowl, cover with boiling water and leave for 30-60 seconds. Drain, cool under cold running water to prevent them from cooking further, then peel off the skin with a sharp knife.

Serving tip

Serve the cobbler with a blueberry milk shake: blend 150g/5oz blueberries, 750ml/1¼ pints milk, four scoops vanilla ice cream and 6 ice cubes in a blender until smooth. Pour into four tall glasses, add a sprig of mint and serve.

BOOZY FLAMBEED BANANAS

USA

Lightly caramelized bananas are served in a liqueur sauce for a dessert of dramatic contrasts – flaming hot seconds before coming to the table, but topped with home-made ice cream.

INGREDIENTS

(Serves 4)

- 1 vanilla pod
- 200ml/7fl oz single cream
- 60g/2½oz caster sugar
- pinch of salt
- 150ml/¼ pint double cream

FOR THE BANANA FLAMBE

- 4 small bananas
- 50g/2oz butter
- 3 tbsp brown sugar
- 2 tsp ground cinnamon
- 4 tbsp banana liqueur
- 4 tbsp Southern Comfort

INGREDIENTS TIP

Instead of the vanilla pod, you could use 1 tsp vanilla essence: stir this into the ice cream mixture before pouring it into the freezer container. Southern Comfort is a unique liqueur spirit, flavoured with oranges, peaches, other exotic fruits and herbs.

1 Slit open the vanilla pod lengthways with a sharp knife and scrape out the seeds. Put the pod, seeds, single cream, caster sugar and salt in a pan. Heat gently until bubbles form on the surface. Remove from heat and cool.

Step 1

2 Meanwhile, put a plastic container in the freezer to chill. Remove the vanilla pod from the mixture, rinse, dry and store for reuse. Whip the double cream until thick and fold in. Pour into the container, cover and freeze for 4 hours.

3 Remove the ice cream from the freezer and allow to soften in the fridge. Peel the bananas and halve lengthways. Melt the butter in a frying pan, add the sugar and cinnamon and stir until the sugar dissolves.

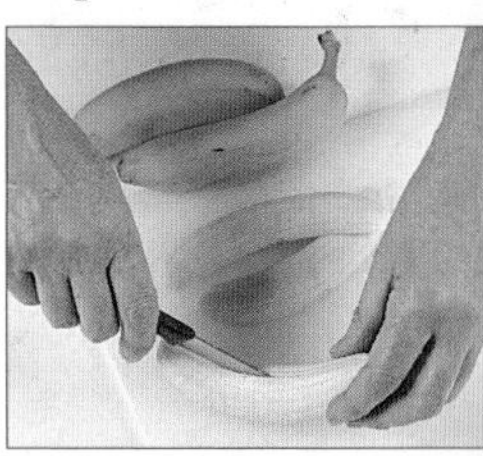

Step 3

4 Add the bananas and fry over a medium heat for 3 minutes, or until the bananas are just soft. Turn over once during cooking and occasionally spoon over the hot juices. Pour over the liqueur and Southern Comfort. Carefully light the alcohol, using a taper. Leave until the flames die down. Put two banana halves, with plenty of the hot juices, onto each plate. Add a scoop of the ice cream and serve.

Step 4

Preparation **30** Min
Freezing **4** Hours
Per Serving: 591 kcal/2464 kJ;
3g protein; 36g fat;
55g carbohydrate

TYPICALLY NEW ORLEANS

New Orleans, in the southern state of Louisiana, is famous for its Mardi Gras festival and its Cajun and Creole cuisine. Southern Comfort, which dates from the 1890s, 'the greatest days of the Old South', was invented in New Orleans and is popular worldwide.

Cooking tips

The ice cream can be prepared well in advance as it will keep for up to 1 month in the freezer • If you want to bring out the taste of vanilla, use the seeds from the pod as well as the pod itself. They give the ice cream a slightly speckled appearance but make the flavour much more intense.

Serving tip

If you have a small table burner, such as a fondue set, you can surprise your guests by cooking the dessert at the table — but warn them to watch out for the flames.

Serving tip Instead of adding the maple syrup to the cream and yoghurt mixture, drizzle it over the top and sprinkle with the nuts. Maple syrup is quite sweet, so add it according to your own taste.

MAPLE SYRUP FRUIT MEDLEY

CANADA

A variety of summer fruits are combined for this vividly coloured dessert that is sweetened with maple syrup, served with a creamy yoghurt sauce and topped with crunchy walnuts.

INGREDIENTS

(Serves 4)

- 200g/7oz raspberries
- 200g/7oz blackberries
- 200g/7oz redcurrants
- 4 small plums
- 1 small peach
- 3 tbsp lemon juice
- 4 tbsp maple syrup
- 1 tart eating apple

FOR THE TOPPING

- 125ml/4fl oz whipping cream
- 125ml/4fl oz natural yoghurt
- 2 tbsp maple syrup
- 2 tbsp finely chopped walnuts

INGREDIENTS TIP

Freeze redcurrants in mid-summer when they are plentiful and least expensive. This way you can use them when blackberries are most prolific later in the summer.

1 Rinse the raspberries and blackberries in a sieve. Separate the redcurrants from their stalks by sliding each sprig carefully between the prongs of a fork.

2 Wash the plums and the peach and pat dry, then cut down along the natural line of each fruit to halve it. Remove the stone and cut the fruit into thin slices.

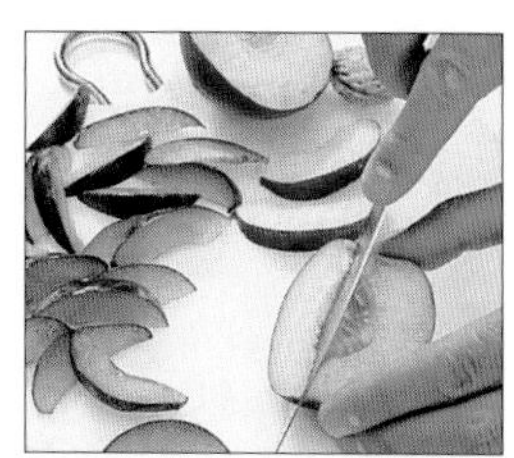

Step 2

3 Mix 2 tablespoons lemon juice with the maple syrup in a large bowl. Cut the apple into quarters and remove the core. Slice thinly, then toss in the remaining lemon juice to prevent the apple from discolouring.

Step 3

4 Add all the fruit to the maple syrup mixture in the bowl and mix together gently. Cover and chill in the fridge for 1 hour.

Step 4

5 Just before serving, whip the cream in a small bowl until thick. Add the yoghurt and the maple syrup and fold them in until evenly mixed.

6 To serve, divide the fruit mixture between four dessert dishes. Add a dollop of the creamy yoghurt mixture and sprinkle with the walnuts.

Preparation **30** Min Chilling **1** Hour
Per Serving: 364 kcal/1523 kJ;
6g protein; 21g fat; 41g carbohydrate

TYPICALLY CANADIAN

Maple syrup is made from the sap of the maple tree. In February and March, holes are bored in the trunk of the trees; the juice is collected, then boiled until reduced to a sweet syrup. Maple flavoured syrup is cheaper than pure syrup, but slightly less flavoursome.

*K*IWI AND STRAWBERRY SALAD

NEW ZEALAND

Aromatic sweet strawberries and brightly coloured kiwi fruit mingle deliciously with a tangy orange syrup to make this eye-catching fruit salad. Toasted almonds add a satisfying crunch.

INGREDIENTS

(Serves 4)

- 8 large strawberries
- 4 kiwi fruit
- 2 tbsp lemon juice
- 2 tbsp runny honey
- 1 tsp vanilla sugar
- pinch of ground cinnamon
- 2 tbsp orange liqueur or fresh orange juice
- 2 tbsp flaked almonds

INGREDIENTS TIP

Vanilla sugar is easy to make yourself and store. Bury one or two vanilla pods in a jar of caster sugar and leave for a couple of days, giving the jar a shake occasionally to distribute the vanilla flavour. Then remove the pods. (They can be reused in another recipe.)

1 Rinse the strawberries in a sieve, drain and pat dry with kitchen paper. Remove the stalks from the strawberries.

2 Peel the kiwi fruit and trim off the tough stalk end. Cut the strawberries and kiwi fruit into 6mm/¼in thick slices.

3 Put the lemon juice, honey, vanilla sugar, ground cinnamon and orange liqueur or fresh orange juice into a small bowl. Use a spoon or fork to blend all of these ingredients evenly.

4 Arrange the sliced strawberries and kiwi fruit in circles on a large serving plate, starting with a layer of kiwi slices. Spoon over the orange syrup. Chill for 1 hour.

5 Place a large frying pan over a medium heat for 1–2 minutes. When the pan is hot, add the flaked almonds and dry-fry, stirring continuously, for 30 seconds, or until the almonds turn light golden-brown, taking care they do not colour too much. Tip the almonds onto a plate. Scatter over the salad and serve immediately.

Step 1

Step 2

Step 3

Preparation **25** Min Chilling **1** Hour
Per Serving: 140 kcal/600 kJ;
3g protein; 4g fat; 24g carbohydrate

TYPICALLY NEW ZEALAND

The small, furry-skinned, egg-shaped kiwi, considered to be New Zealand's national fruit, actually originated in China. New Zealanders adopted the fruit, previously called the Chinese gooseberry, as their own and named it after their national bird, the kiwi.

COOKING TIP

Buy kiwi fruit that are ripe but not too soft. The flesh should yield slightly when squeezed gently. Hard, unripe kiwi fruit can be ripened by leaving them, together with an apple, in a plastic bag at room temperature. The apple gives off enzymes that speed up the ripening process.

SERVING TIP

Serve this fruit salad with a selection of plain and milk chocolate dessert biscuits and vanilla ice cream or a spoonful of rich crème fraîche.

3 WAYS WITH MELONS

Melon shells make ideal bowls for fruity fillings. Here are three decorative variations from around the world – they look exotic but are simple to prepare.

MELON IN HONEY CREAM

Preparation: **40** Min Chilling: **2** Hours

TURKEY

(SERVES 4)

- ½ watermelon
- 6mm/¼in piece root ginger
- 1 tbsp lemon juice
- 1 tsp runny honey

FOR THE CREAM

- 1 tbsp powdered gelatine
- juice of ½ lemon
- 4 tsp runny honey
- 284ml/10fl oz double cream
- 150ml/¼ pint white wine or white grape juice

1 Remove the watermelon seeds, then scoop out the flesh with a melon baller. Cut a sliver of skin off the bottom of the melon half so that it stands upright.

2 Peel the ginger, chop very finely and mix with 1 tablespoon lemon juice, honey and melon balls.

3 Sprinkle the gelatine over the lemon juice in a small bowl and dissolve by standing the bowl over a pan of simmering water. Lift out the bowl and stir in the honey. Whip the cream until thick, then gradually whisk in the wine. Fold in the gelatine.

4 Put half the melon ball mixture and juice in the melon shell. Cover with cream. Cover and chill for 2 hours. Serve with the rest of the melon balls on top.

PROVENC

Preparation: **45**

FRANCE

(SERVES 4)

- 2 small Charentais melons
- 100g/4oz black grapes
- 100g/4oz green grapes
- 2 small figs
- 1 kiwi fruit
- 1 tbsp lemon juice
- 1 tbsp fresh orange juice
- 25g/1oz caster sugar
- 125ml/4fl oz white wine
- 2 tsp flaked almonds

1 With a small, sharp knife, cut the melons in half with zigzag cuts. Remove seeds and scoop out some of the melon flesh with a melon baller. Take

Melon and Orange Flamenco

Preparation: **20** Min Chilling: **2** Hours

Spain

(SERVES 4)

- 2 small honeydew melons
- 4–6 tbsp ginger conserve
- juice of ½ lemon
- 1 orange
- 2 tsp flaked almonds
- a few mint sprigs

1 Cut the melons in half, remove the seeds and scoop out the flesh with a spoon. Cut a piece of skin off the bottom of each melon half so that it stands upright.

2 Dice the melon flesh. Purée a quarter of the diced flesh in a blender with the ginger conserve, to taste, and lemon juice. Pour into a bowl, add the melon pieces, cover and chill for 2 hours. Wrap the melon shells and chill.

3 Peel the orange, removing all the white pith and cut into segments. Remove the pips.

4 Heat a dry frying pan over a low heat. Add the almonds and stir until they are lightly browned. Tip out of the pan onto a plate and reserve.

5 Stir the melon mixture well, then spoon into the melon halves. Arrange the orange segments on top and decorate with the almonds and mint sprigs. Serve immediately.

Melon Baskets

Chilling: **1** Hour

care to keep the edge intact. Cut a piece of skin off the base of each melon so it stands upright.

2 Pull the grapes from the stalks, cut in half and remove the seeds. Trim and dice the figs. Peel and dice the kiwi fruit.

3 Mix the lemon and orange juice with the sugar and wine (use white grape juice, if preferred). Add all the fruit, stir, cover and chill for 1 hour.

4 Brown the almonds in a dry frying pan over a low heat for 1 minute. Fill the melon halves with the fruit. Sprinkle with the almonds and serve.

STICKY COCONUT RICE WITH MANGO AND PAPAYA

THAILAND

Until recently the delights of Thai cooking were a well-kept secret. Once you've tasted the sweet coconut-flavoured rice and slices of tropical fruit, this dish will always be on the menu.

INGREDIENTS

(Serves 4)

- 75g/3oz sticky or short-grain rice
- 50g/2oz creamed coconut
- 50g/2oz caster sugar
- 1 small papaya (pawpaw)
- 1 small mango
- ½ tsp rose water, optional
- 4 tbsp pineapple or orange juice

TO DECORATE

- 1 lime
- 8 pecan nut halves

INGREDIENTS TIP

Sticky rice, often called glutinous rice, is available from specialist oriental shops. Short-grain or pudding rice is a good substitute for sticky rice. Both absorb the water as the grains cook and become soft and sticky.

1 Rinse the rice in a sieve and place in a medium-sized saucepan. Cover with water and bring to the boil. Cover the pan and cook over a medium heat for 15 minutes, or until the rice is tender.

Step 1

2 Grate or finely dice the creamed coconut. Place in a bowl, pour over 90ml/3fl oz hot water and stir until smooth. Add the sugar and mix well. Stir 2–3 tablespoons of the coconut syrup into the cooked rice, cover and leave to cool for 1 hour.

3 Cut the papaya in half and remove the seeds with a spoon. Peel the papaya halves and cut the flesh into thin slices. Peel the mango and carefully cut the flesh away from the stone, then cut into thin slices.

Step 3

4 Combine rose-water, if using, with the pineapple or orange juice in a bowl. Add the mango and papaya pieces. Pare shreds of rind from the lime with a citrus zester.

Step 4

5 Arrange the fruit and rice in small dishes. Add 1 tablespoon water to the remaining coconut syrup and spoon over. Garnish with the lime shreds and pecans.

Preparation **35** Min Cooling **1** Hour
Per Serving: 253 kcal/1064 kJ;
3g protein; 10g fat; 42g carbohydrate

TYPICALLY THAI

Rice is a staple food in Thailand. It is a very versatile ingredient and is used in many dishes from main courses with chicken and seafood to fruity desserts. Tropical Thailand produces an abundance of fresh fruit, including papayas and over a dozen different varieties of mango.

Cooking tip

Coconut syrup can be made with home-made coconut milk instead of creamed coconut: pour 200ml/7fl oz hot water over 200g/7oz desiccated coconut; stir well and leave to stand for 20 minutes, then drain the liquid by straining through a sieve lined with a cloth. At step 2, leave out the water and stir in the sugar.

Serving tip

To set the scene for this fragrant dessert, make a wonderful table centre-piece using exotic fresh fruit or decorate place settings with attractive flowers.

CHINESE TOFFEE APPLES

CHINA

INGREDIENTS
(Serves 4)

- 8 very small, firm eating apples (about 700g/1½lb)
- 1 litre/1¾ pints soya oil, for frying
- 75g/3oz caster sugar
- 2 tbsp sesame seeds

FOR THE BATTER
- 1 egg
- 50g/2oz plain flour
- 50g/2oz cornflour

INGREDIENTS TIP
Instead of soya oil, any other oil with a mild flavour could be substituted. Corn, vegetable or groundnut oil would all be suitable. After using the oil, leave it to cool, then strain it back into the bottle through a very fine sieve, using a metal or plastic funnel.

Coated in batter, deep-fried and drizzled with golden caramel, these sweet apples are a favourite in the city of Peking – and enjoyed worldwide by everyone who loves Chinese food.

1 To make the batter, put the egg, flour, cornflour and 4 tablespoons cold water in a large bowl. Beat well with a wooden spoon to form a smooth batter.

2 Peel the apples and, keeping them whole, remove the cores. Put the apples in the batter and turn until completely coated. Leave them in the batter until ready to cook.

3 Heat the oil in a large, heavy-based pan to 190°C/375°F. If you don't have a cooking thermometer, test the temperature by carefully dipping the handle of a wooden spoon into the oil – small bubbles should form around it.

4 Add the coated apples to the oil, two at a time, and fry for about 3 minutes until golden brown. Remove them with a slotted spoon and drain on kitchen paper. Remove the pan from the heat.

5 Place 1 tablespoon of the oil in a clean frying pan. Add the sugar and heat gently, stirring until it melts and turns pale golden.

6 Place two apples on each plate and quickly pour over the caramel. Sprinkle with sesame seeds and serve immediately.

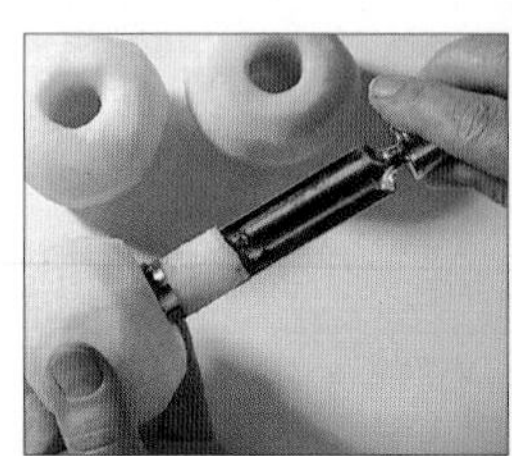

Step 2

Step 2

Step 3

Preparation **30** Min Frying **10** Min
Per Serving: 648 kcal/2684 kJ;
2g protein; 60g fat; 27g carbohydrate

TYPICALLY PEKINESE
Surprising though it may seem, wheat is a commonly used ingredient in Pekinese cooking and is almost as popular as the familiar Chinese staple, rice. Many varieties of noodle, as well as most batters for fried foods, are made from wheat flour.

Cooking tips

If small apples are unavailable, use large ones cored and cut into quarters before frying. Suitable apple varieties for this dish include Cox's Orange Pippin, Sturmer Pippin and Royal Gala • When stirring the caramel, use a wooden spoon as the heat of the caramel will melt a plastic one.

Serving tip

In China, tea accompanies every meal, from starter to dessert. Fragrant jasmine tea, served without milk or sugar, would go particularly well with these sweet toffee apples.

SERVING TIP You could serve the sorbet in lemon cases: use 4 lemons, wash, cut the tops off and carefully remove the flesh. Fill the cases with the sorbet and chill before serving.

PERSIAN ORANGE SORBET

IRAN

This refreshing and colourful orange sorbet is sprinkled with dates and pistachio nuts. It is a wonderful dish that must have been made for balmy Arabian nights.

INGREDIENTS

(Serves 4)

- 3 oranges
- 75g/3oz caster sugar
- 1 tbsp runny honey
- 2 tbsp lemon juice

TO DECORATE

- 4 fresh dates
- 4 tsp chopped pistachio nuts

INGREDIENTS TIP

Fresh dates from Israel and California tend to be more readily available in winter months and are sweet and succulent. The finest variety are called Medjool and have plump flesh and a soft skin. Dried dates can be used instead; they are sweeter and stickier than fresh but are available all year round from most supermarkets.

1 Wash the oranges thoroughly in hot water and dry with kitchen paper. Grate the rind with a fine grater. Cut the oranges in half and squeeze out the juice.

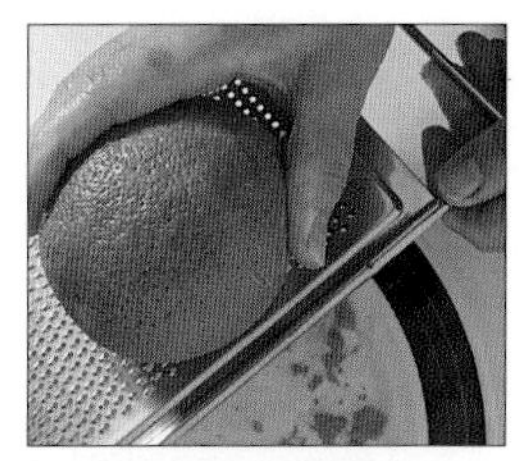

Step 1

2 Combine the orange rind, juice, sugar and honey in a small saucepan. Cook over a moderate heat, stirring all the time, until the sugar has dissolved.

Step 2

3 Remove the orange syrup from the heat and stir in the lemon juice. Pour into a heatproof jug and leave until cold, then transfer to a plastic container and put in the freezer. Once ice crystals start to form, remove from the freezer and whisk with a balloon whisk or electric hand whisk. Freeze until the sorbet is firm. This will take about 4 hours.

4 While the sorbet is freezing, wash the dates and pat dry. Remove the stones and finely slice the flesh. Put four dessert plates into the fridge to chill.

Step 4

5 Whisk the sorbet vigorously, once again, then arrange in scoops on the chilled plates with the date slices. Sprinkle with the chopped pistachio nuts and serve.

Preparation **20** Min Chilling **4** Hours

Per Serving: 134 kcal/569 kJ; 0.5g protein; 0.1g fat; 34g carbohydrate

TYPICALLY IRANIAN

Oranges were brought to Persia, the old name for Iran, from China and today are grown on large plantations. They are a very popular ingredient in dishes ranging from milk puddings to rice pilafs and sweet pastries.

ORANGE AND AVOCADO FRUIT SALAD

ISRAEL

In the Middle East, avocados are served in both sweet and savoury dishes. Here, juicy orange segments are the perfect foil to their buttery flesh, while fresh dates add a rich sweetness.

INGREDIENTS

(Serves 4)

- 3 large oranges
- about 125ml/4fl oz fresh orange juice
- 2 tbsp caster sugar
- pinch of ground star anise
- pinch of ground cinnamon
- 1 avocado
- 2–3 tbsp lemon juice
- 60g/2½oz fresh dates

INGREDIENTS TIP

Star anise is the fruit and seed pod of an evergreen tree and resembles a small, reddish-brown star with a seed in each point. Used whole, it makes an attractive garnish for a dish, as well as adding an aniseed flavour. It is used in Chinese cooking to flavour meat and poultry and is one of the spices that make up five spice powder.

1 Wash and dry the oranges. Using a cannelle knife or citrus zester, pare strips of rind from one orange. Alternatively, cut the peel off in very thin pieces and slice into fine strips. Slice the orange in half and squeeze the juice. Add extra fresh orange juice to make the quantity up to 250ml/9fl oz.

2 Peel the remaining two oranges, removing all the white pith. Slice down each side of each segment and detach the flesh from the membrane. Remove any pips.

Step 2

3 Heat the orange juice, rind, sugar, star anise and cinnamon gently in a small pan. Cook for 10–15 minutes, stirring occasionally, until the mixture thickens and reduces to a syrup.

Step 3

4 Cut the avocado in half and prise out the stone. Peel and cut across into thin slices. Sprinkle with lemon juice immediately to prevent discoloration.

Step 4

5 Arrange the orange segments and avocado slices on four serving plates and pour over the orange syrup. Wash the dates, cut in half and remove the stone. Slice into strips and sprinkle over the salad.

Preparation **45** Min Cooking **15** Min
Per Serving: 143 kcal/602 kJ;
2g protein; 5g fat; 24g carbohydrate

TYPICALLY ISRAELI

Fruit and vegetable markets in Israel are noisy, bustling places and the Israeli cook has a huge choice of locally grown produce for making dishes such as latkes (grated potato cakes), tabbouleh (a salad of fresh herbs and bulgar wheat) and slow-cooked stews.

COOKING TIP

To test if an avocado is ripe, cradle the fruit in the palm of your hand and squeeze it gently – it should give to light pressure. The ripening process can be speeded up by storing avocados in a warm place. Once ripe, avocados will keep for about 8 days if stored somewhere cool.

SERVING TIP

Crisp almond biscuits, such as macaroons or Italian amaretti, make an attractive and tasty accompaniment to this fruit salad.

SCOTTISH CREAM CROWDIE

GREAT BRITAIN

This luscious dessert derives its name from a thin porridge made with oatmeal. Here, the oatmeal is toasted to give a deliciously crunchy texture to the honey-sweetened cream.

INGREDIENTS

(Serves 4)

- 2 tbsp medium oatmeal
- 250ml/9oz whipping cream
- 5 tbsp runny honey
- 2 tbsp whisky (optional)
- 500g/1lb 2oz fresh raspberries

FOR THE TOPPING

- ½ tbsp butter
- 4 tbsp oat flakes

INGREDIENTS TIP

Buy oatmeal in small quantities as oats contain a lot of fat and go rancid quickly. Porridge oats, widely available in supermarkets, can be used in both the recipe and for the topping. Rolled oats are the same as porridge oats, but porridge oats is now the more commonly used name.

1 Toast the oatmeal in a dry frying pan over a medium heat for 2–3 minutes, or until lightly browned; do not let it burn. Turn onto a plate and leave to cool.

Step 1

2 Whip the cream with a balloon whisk, or an electric hand whisk, until soft peaks begin to form. Warm the honey gently until liquid and stir in the whisky. Fold into the cream with the cooled toasted oatmeal.

Step 2

3 Rinse the raspberries in a colander, taking care not to damage the delicate fruit. Drain well and gently pat dry with kitchen paper. Pull off any stalks.

4 Place a few raspberries in the base of four tall dessert glasses and cover with a layer of the cream mixture. Repeat this layering process, finishing with a layer of cream, topped with 2 or 3 raspberries. Chill for 2 hours.

Step 4

5 Melt the butter gently in a small frying pan but do not let it brown. Add the oat flakes, fry briefly until just golden, then remove from the pan and leave to cool. Sprinkle over the dessert just before serving.

Preparation **20** Min Chilling **2** Hours
Per Serving: 474 kcal/1971 kJ;
3g protein; 38g fat; 26g carbohydrate

TYPICALLY SCOTTISH

Barley and peat, crystal clear water and a cool climate are the basic requirements for whisky, the Scots' 'water of life'. True malt whiskies are matured for 10–12 years in wood casks, which give the spirit its characteristic golden hue.

Cooking tip

Toasting oatmeal makes it an attractive golden brown and gives it a slightly nutty flavour. It is not necessary to add fat to the pan as the oatmeal won't stick, but stir frequently to prevent burning. Tip the oatmeal onto a plate as soon as it is the desired colour as, if left in the pan, it will continue to brown and may burn.

Serving tip

For extra colour, decorate each dessert with a sprig of fresh mint. Alternatively, for a nutty topping, use flaked almonds or chopped pistachio nuts instead of the oat flakes.

*T*RADITIONAL ENGLISH TRIFLE

GREAT BRITAIN

Trifle is the quintessential English party dessert, especially at Christmas. However, the sponge, fresh fruit, jelly, smooth custard and sherry make it a favourite at any celebration.

INGREDIENTS

(Serves 4)

- 6 ripe peaches or 415g/14½oz can peach halves
- 250g/9oz strawberries
- 1 box of 8 trifle sponges
- 2 tbsp strawberry jam
- 200ml/7fl oz sweet sherry or orange juice
- 1 packet orange jelly

FOR THE CUSTARD

- 4 tbsp custard powder
- 1.2 litres/2 pints milk
- 2 tbsp caster sugar

FOR THE TOPPING

- 200ml/7fl oz whipping cream
- 2 tbsp caster sugar

INGREDIENTS TIP

To save time, use 600ml/1 pint of ready-made thick custard available in cartons or cans and spoon straight over the fruit without heating.

1 If using fresh peaches, cover with boiling water for 1 minute, drain and rinse under cold water. Peel and cut in half. Remove the stones and cut the flesh into cubes. If using canned peaches, drain and cut into cubes.

Step 1

2 Reserve 3–4 of the best strawberries. Remove the stalks from the remaining berries and cut each strawberry in half. Cut the sponges into 4cm/1¾in cubes, halve, and spread with the jam. Sandwich the two halves together again. Place in a glass serving bowl and pour over the sherry or juice.

Step 2

3 Make the jelly following the packet instructions but use only three-quarters of the water recommended. Cool until syrupy but not set. Arrange the fruit on the sponge and pour over the jelly. Chill in the fridge until set.

Step 3

4 Make the custard with the milk and sugar, following the instructions. While still warm, pour over fruit. Leave until cold.

5 Whip cream and sugar until soft peaks form. Spread three-quarters over the trifle. Whip the remaining cream until thick and pipe into rosettes on top. Halve the reserved strawberries and use to decorate.

Preparation **40** Min Chilling **1** Hour
Per Serving: 256 kcal/1079 kJ;
6g protein; 10g fat; 34g carbohydrate

TYPICALLY ENGLISH

Trifle, also known as tipsy cake because of the sherry content, was a great favourite in Victorian England. It was always served in a cut glass bowl at Christmas gatherings. A glass dish is ideal for displaying the colourful layers of this luxurious dessert to best advantage.

Cooking tip

You can prepare the trifle, up to Step 4, the day before. Cover the bowl tightly with cling film and store in the fridge. About 30 minutes before serving, take it out of the fridge, whip the cream, spread over the trifle and decorate with cream rosettes and the remaining strawberry halves.

Serving tip

Sherry, especially a dry one, is generally drunk as an aperitif. But a medium or sweet sherry makes a good dessert wine too – serve a glass with the trifle.

SUMMER PUDDING

GREAT BRITAIN

This classic fruit pudding makes the most of home-grown English soft fruits and currants – their sweet flavour and jewel-like colours providing a feast for the eye and the palate.

INGREDIENTS

(Serves 6)

- 700g/1½lb mixed soft summer fruits (strawberries, raspberries, blackberries, blackcurrants, redcurrants)
- 60g/2½oz caster sugar
- ½ tsp ground cinnamon
- 1 tbsp lemon juice
- 6–8 slices white bread

TO DECORATE

- soft summer fruits
- mint sprigs

INGREDIENTS TIP

Slice the bread from an uncut loaf an hour or so before using so the slices dry out a little. This will make them more porous. Ready-sliced bread in plastic bags is not suitable as it is not absorbent enough to take up the fruit juices properly.

1 Remove stalks or leaves from fruit and discard any that are bruised. Rinse in a colander under cold running water. Place in a saucepan with sugar, cinnamon and juice.

2 Simmer for 5–10 minutes until the fruits start to soften and the juices run. Set aside and allow to cool.

Step 2

3 Cut the crusts from the bread and use the slices to line the base and side of a 1.5 litre/2½ pint pudding basin. Cut the bread as needed so it fits tightly and trim level with the top of the basin. Reserve the leftover slices.

Step 3

4 Spoon the fruit and enough of the juices into the bowl so the bread is thoroughly moistened. Reserve the rest of the juice. Cover the pudding with the reserved bread, trimming it to fit. Cover with cling film and place a plate on top that fits inside the rim.

Step 4

5 Place a weight on the plate and chill for at least 24 hours but no more than 2 days. To serve, turn the pudding out onto a serving plate and cover any white patches of bread by spooning over the reserved juice. Decorate with the soft summer fruits and mint sprigs. Dust with icing sugar.

Preparation **30** Min
Cooking **5-10** Min
Chilling **24** Hours
Per Serving: 146 kcal/625 kJ
3g protein; 0.6g fat;
34g carbohydrate

TYPICALLY ENGLISH

The southern English counties are famous for their soft fruit. Strawberries are the first to come into season and these arrive in June in time for the Wimbledon Championships where a bowl of strawberries and cream is almost as popular as the tennis!

Serving tip Traditionally, serve the summer pudding with a generous splash of pouring cream. Alternatively, serve with a scoop or two of your favourite ice cream.

SERVING TIP These fritters make an excellent evening snack. They taste delicious served with coffee or hot chocolate and a generous helping of vanilla ice cream or whipped cream.

SWISS CHERRY FRITTERS

SWITZERLAND

INGREDIENTS

(Serves 4)

- 2 eggs
- 175g/6oz plain flour
- 200ml/7fl oz white wine or white grape juice
- 1 tbsp caster sugar
- pinch of salt
- 275g/10oz cherries
- 1 litre/1¾ pints sunflower oil, for frying
- 1 tbsp ground cinnamon
- 6 tbsp icing sugar

INGREDIENTS TIP

Choose cherries with their stalks on. The cherries can be stoned, if you prefer, but do this from the side of the fruit so the stalks remain attached.

These 'Beignets aux Cerises', made from juicy, sweet cherries dipped in batter and fried until crisp and golden, are easy to make, great fun to eat – and delicious too.

1 Separate the eggs and put the egg whites on one side. Combine the egg yolks with the flour, wine or juice, caster sugar and salt and stir well to make a smooth batter. Cover and leave to rest for 30 minutes.

Step 1

2 Wash and dry the cherries. Stone, if wished. Tie bundles of 3 or 4 cherries together by their stalks, using thin string.

3 Heat the oil in a deep-fat fryer or deep saucepan to 190°C/375°F. To test the temperature, dip the handle of a wooden spoon into the fat – small bubbles should form around the handle.

Step 4

4 Beat the egg whites until they form soft peaks and gently fold them into the batter. Using a fork, dip the cherry bundles one by one into the batter. Lift out and put straight into the hot oil. Fry for 2–3 minutes until they just turn golden brown.

Step 5

5 Lift the fritters out of the fat with a slotted spoon and place on kitchen paper to drain. Mix the cinnamon with the icing sugar and sprinkle generously over the fritters. Serve while still warm.

Preparation **15** Min Cooking **20** Min
Resting **30** Min
Per Serving: 409 kcal/1725 kJ;
8g protein; 11g fat; 68g carbohydrate

TYPICALLY SWISS

Cherry trees grow all along the sweeping valleys that surround Lake Lucerne in central Switzerland and the mass of pink blossom in early spring heralds the arrival of warmer weather. Cherries are used in many Swiss desserts and also distilled as liqueurs.

TIPSY STRAWBERRIES ROMANOV

UKRAINE

Soaking strawberries in vodka adds a new dimension to their sweet and aromatic juice. With its light cheese topping, this is a simple and elegant version of strawberries and cream.

INGREDIENTS
(Serves 4)

- 500g/1lb 2oz strawberries
- 1 small orange
- 4 tbsp vodka
- 3 tbsp caster sugar

FOR THE TOPPING

- 142ml/5fl oz whipping cream
- 25g/1oz caster sugar
- 200g/7oz low-fat soft cheese or curd cheese
- 4–5 tbsp milk

INGREDIENTS TIP

Because of its high alcohol content, vodka does not freeze, so a bottle can be stored in the freezer. Here, brandy or an orange liqueur could be used instead of vodka. For a non-alcoholic option, use extra orange juice or elderflower cordial.

1 Wash the strawberries, reserving four with the stalk left on. Pull the stalks from the strawberries and cut into halves or quarters.

2 Rinse the orange in hot water and dry on kitchen paper. Using a cannelle knife, peel off thin strips of the rind. Halve the orange and squeeze the juice.

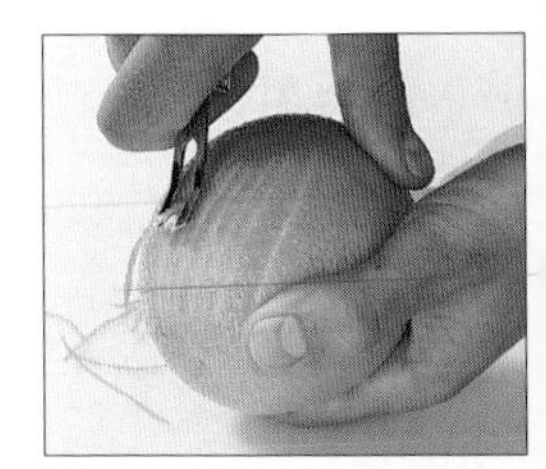

Step 2

3 Mix together the orange juice, vodka and sugar in a bowl and stir until the sugar has dissolved. Toss the strawberries in the mixture, cover and chill in the fridge for at least 1 hour for the flavours to blend.

Step 3

4 While the strawberries are soaking, whip the cream until soft peaks form and stir in the caster sugar. Soften the cheese by beating it in a bowl, then fold in the cream. Beat in the milk a spoonful at a time, until you have a smooth consistency. Store in the fridge until required.

Step 4

5 To serve, place the strawberries and juice in four dessert bowls. Spoon some of the creamy cheese on top and decorate with the reserved whole strawberries. Scatter the shredded orange rind over and serve the remaining creamy cheese separately.

Preparation **30** Min Chilling **1** Hour
Per Serving: 410 kcal/1712 kJ;
4g protein; 22g fat; 45g carbohydrate

TYPICALLY UKRAINIAN

Vodka, the traditional Ukrainian drink, was originally made from potatoes, but is now distilled from wheat.The Ukrainian people are renowned for their excellent cooking, much of which is based on the abundance of fruit and vegetables produced in their country.

Cooking tip

Appearances can be deceptive – large attractive-looking strawberries are often far less sweet and less aromatic than smaller ones. The strawberries can be left to soak in the vodka for much longer if you prefer – simply cover the bowl tightly with non-PVC cling film and store in the fridge for up to 12 hours.

Serving tip

Add small squares of sponge cake or coarsely crumbled sponge-finger biscuits to the serving dishes before adding the strawberries or hand the biscuits round separately.

*P*LUM COMPOTE

GERMANY

Enjoy an autumnal fruit compote that combines deep blue-skinned plums with golden apricots. Cinnamon and plum brandy turn this dessert into a grown-up treat.

INGREDIENTS

(Serves 4)

- 400g/14oz ripe plums
- 200g/7oz apricots
- 1 lemon
- 50g/2oz sugar cubes
- 1 cinnamon stick
- 2 tbsp plum brandy

FOR THE TOPPING

- 200ml/7oz whipping cream
- 25g/1oz caster sugar
- 2-3 tbsp plum brandy

INGREDIENTS TIP

Choose plums and apricots with a sweet, fresh smell. They should be sufficiently ripe, but not too soft, or the compote will lack flavour and aroma. You can use plain brandy instead of plum brandy if you wish, or use red grape or cranberry juice for a non-alcoholic alternative.

1 Wash the plums and apricots, cut them in half and remove the stone. Cut the fruit halves into thick slices.

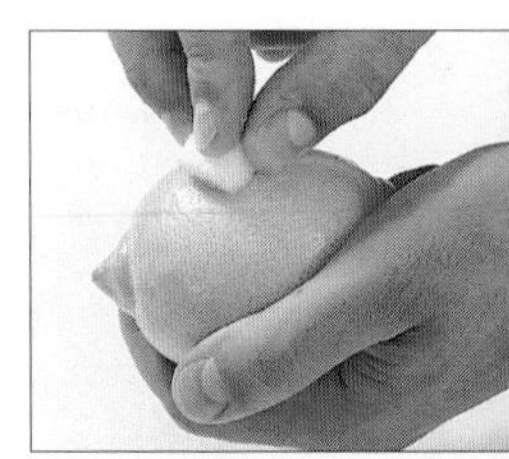

Step 2

2 Wash the lemon in hot water and dry. Rub the sugar cubes over the rind – the sugar will absorb the sharp lemon flavour. Cut the lemon in half and squeeze the juice. Dissolve the sugar cubes in 2 tablespoons water in a pan over a gentle heat. Turn up the heat and boil until the syrup turns light caramel.

Step 2

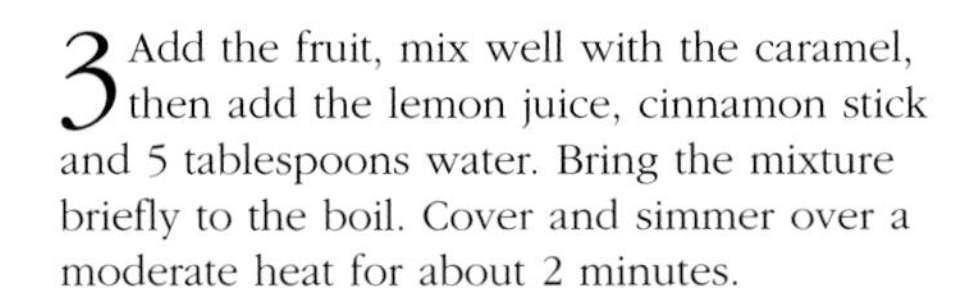

3 Add the fruit, mix well with the caramel, then add the lemon juice, cinnamon stick and 5 tablespoons water. Bring the mixture briefly to the boil. Cover and simmer over a moderate heat for about 2 minutes.

4 Stir 2 tablespoons plum brandy into the compote and leave to cool. Cover and chill in the fridge for at least 3 hours.

Step 4

5 Whip the cream until soft peaks form. Fold in the caster sugar and plum brandy to taste. Remove the cinnamon stick from the compote and divide the fruit mixture evenly between four dishes. Add a scoop of whipped cream to each portion and serve.

Preparation **30** Min Chilling **3** Hours
Per Serving: 390 kcal/1624 kJ;
2g protein; 24g fat; 33g carbohydrate

TYPICALLY GERMAN

Any variety of plum is suitable for this dish but Bühler plums, which grow in the Bühl Valley, are traditionally used. Bühler plums are particularly juicy, round instead of oval and delicious raw. They are used in sweet and savoury dishes and made into plum brandy.

Cooking tip

If you enjoy the taste of plum brandy but want to avoid alcohol, stir the brandy into the fruit mixture before bringing it to the boil. During boiling, the alcohol evaporates but the fruit retains the potent aroma of the spirit.

Serving tip

Serve with warm pancakes: whisk 4 egg whites with 100g/4oz caster sugar until stiff. Mix 4 egg yolks with 150g/5oz sour cream and 100g/4oz plain flour. Stir well to make a smooth batter, fold in the egg whites and fry until the pancakes are set.

*F*RUIT CAROUSEL WITH WINE

GERMANY

Made with a mixture of colourful fruits, this dramatic fruit salad is particularly eye-catching. Dessert wine mellows some of the more tangy fruits, making them sweet and luscious.

INGREDIENTS

(Serves 4)

- 2 small lemons
- 25g/1oz caster sugar
- 150ml/¼ pint muscat wine or white grape juice
- 1 tart eating apple
- 2 small kiwi fruit
- 100g/4oz green grapes
- 2 ripe nectarines
- 200g/7oz redcurrants
- 100g/4oz strawberries
- 4 scoops vanilla ice cream, to serve

INGREDIENTS TIP

Vary the fruit according to what is in season if you wish to use all fresh produce. Alternatively, if nectarines are unavailable, you can use canned peach slices but drain well before adding them to the fruit salad.

1 Wash the lemons thoroughly under hot running water, then dry. Grate the rind and squeeze the juice. Combine the rind and juice with the sugar and wine and mix well.

Step 1

2 Cut the apple into quarters, peel and core. Slice the quarters thinly and toss immediately in the lemon mixture to prevent them from discolouring.

Step 2

3 Peel the kiwi fruit, halve and cut into thin slices. Wash the grapes and pull from their stalks. Cut them in half and remove the pips with the tip of a small knife. Peel and halve the nectarines, discard the stones and cut into thin slices.

4 Wash the redcurrants and pull the fruit from the stalks with the prongs of a fork. Wash the strawberries, pull the stalks off and cut in half. Remove the apple slices from the lemon juice.

Step 4

5 Layer the fruits in a large bowl, then pour over the lemon and wine mixture. Leave to stand for 30 minutes for the flavours to develop. Serve with vanilla ice cream.

Preparation **30** Min Standing **30** Min
Per Serving: 221 kcal/936 kJ;
4g protein; 3g fat; 40g carbohydrate

TYPICALLY GERMAN

The Viktualienmarkt in Munich is famous for its amazing array of fresh fruit and vegetables. The Germans preserve layers of soft fruits in rum as they come into season. Once the fruits are bottled the jar is sealed until Christmas when the 'Rumtoft' is eaten.

Cooking tip

This dish can be prepared in advance, but make sure the fruits are tossed in the lemon and wine mixture after they have been cut, to avoid discoloration. Store in the fridge, removing half an hour before serving. This allows the fruit to return to room temperature and regain its flavour after chilling.

Serving tip

To decorate, sprinkle with chopped hazelnuts or walnuts. Don't forget nuts are a good dessert accompaniment – put a dish of mixed nuts on the table with nutcrackers for your guests to crack their own.

AUSTRIAN APPLE DOUGHNUTS

AUSTRIA

One of Austria's favourite desserts, this sweet, crisp treat is simply mouth-watering. The crunchy cinnamon coating contrasts with the juicy apple hidden inside – these doughnuts have star quality.

INGREDIENTS

(Serves 4)

- 125g/4½oz plain flour
- 125ml/4fl oz white wine or water
- pinch of salt
- 2 eggs
- 2 tbsp butter
- 1 tbsp brandy
- 3 large eating apples
- 3 tbsp lemon juice
- 2 tbsp rum (optional)
- 125g/4½oz caster sugar
- 1 tsp ground cinnamon
- 1 litre/1¾ pints sunflower oil

FOR THE CUSTARD

- 2 tbsp custard powder
- 600ml/1 pint milk
- 1 tbsp caster sugar

INGREDIENTS TIP

Choose an apple variety with a slightly tart flavour and firm, crisp texture. Granny Smith, Cox and Russet apples would all be good.

1 Mix the flour with the wine and salt in a mixing bowl to form a smooth batter. Separate the eggs and melt the butter. Stir the egg yolks, butter and brandy into the batter. Cover and leave to stand for 1 hour.

Step 1

2 Peel and core the apples. Cut them into 1cm/½in slices, then sprinkle with the lemon juice and rum, if using. Mix the sugar and cinnamon together and sprinkle half over the apple slices. Stand for 30 minutes.

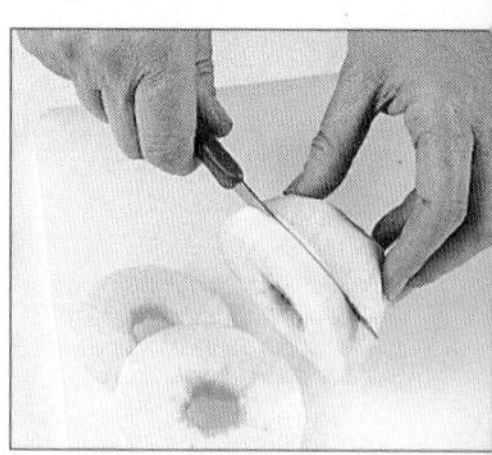

Step 2

3 Whisk the egg whites until soft peaks form and fold into the batter. Prepare the custard with the milk and sugar following the packet instructions, then leave to cool.

4 Heat the oil in a large saucepan to 190°C/375°F. To check it is hot enough, dip the handle of a wooden spoon in the oil. Small bubbles should appear around it.

5 Dip the apple slices into the batter a few at a time and deep fry for about 3 minutes until golden brown. Drain on kitchen paper, then sprinkle with the remaining cinnamon and sugar. Serve hot with the custard.

Step 5

Preparation **1** Hour Cooking **30** Min
Standing **1½** Hours
Per Serving: 788 kcal/3296 kJ;
11g protein; 38g fat; 75g carbohydrate

TYPICALLY AUSTRIAN

Fruit desserts have long been popular in Austria - cookery books that have survived from the 15th and 16th centuries contain fruit recipes which are still favourites today. Apples feature in other famous Austrian delicacies, such as the pastry dessert, apple strudel.

COOKING TIP

When deep frying any food, it is important to heat the oil to the correct temperature – 190°C/375°F. Too hot and the coating will burn before the inside is done, too cool and the coating will absorb oil and become soggy. If you enjoy deep-fried food, it is worth investing in a cooking thermometer.

SERVING TIP

Instead of serving the doughnuts with custard or cream, offer a selection of ice cream. Try one scoop of crunchy walnut ice cream and one of vanilla with each serving.

PEARS BELLE HELENE

NORTHERN FRANCE

Pear halves gently poached in syrup and served with vanilla ice cream and a warm chocolate sauce make an elegant dessert that rounds off any occasion with a flourish.

INGREDIENTS

(Serves 4)

- ½ vanilla pod
- 50g/2oz caster sugar
- 2 ripe pears
- 50g/2oz dark chocolate or mocha chocolate
- 2 tbsp double cream
- 4 scoops vanilla ice cream
- a few sprigs of lemon balm, to decorate

INGREDIENTS TIP

When buying the pears, make sure the fruit is ripe and aromatic but not too soft. Williams or Conference pears are both good choices. Lemon balm, a member of the mint family, has a mild, citrus flavour and aroma and can be used in marinades, fruit drinks and stuffings.

1 Slit the vanilla pod lengthways and scrape out the seeds with the tip of a small knife. Combine the pod, seeds and sugar with 125ml/4fl oz water in a wide pan. Bring to the boil, stirring, over a medium heat.

2 Halve the pears lengthways and, using a spoon, carefully remove the cores. Peel the pear halves. Add to the vanilla syrup. Cover and simmer for about 5 minutes, or until the pears are tender.

Step 2

3 Remove the pan from the heat and leave to cool slightly. Transfer the pears and syrup to a dish and chill for at least 2 hours.

4 Bring a little water to the boil in a small saucepan. Coarsely chop the chocolate and put it, together with the cream, in a bowl, then stand the bowl in the saucepan. Stir until the chocolate has melted. Remove the bowl from the pan.

Step 4

5 Remove the pears from the syrup and drain well. Arrange one pear half and one scoop of ice cream on individual serving plates. Spoon over the chocolate sauce and decorate with lemon balm sprigs.

Step 5

Preparation **30** Min Chilling **2** Hours
Per Serving: 256 kcal/1076 kJ;
2g protein; 11g fat; 39g carbohydrate

TYPICALLY FRENCH

'Poire Belle Hélène' was first served in Paris in 1864. This dish of poached pears coated in a rich chocolate sauce was specially created in honour of the first performance of Jacques Offenbach's opera 'La Belle Hélène'. Today it is still considered a true gourmet recipe.

Cooking tip

To melt the chocolate and cream in a microwave, place both ingredients in a small microwave-proof bowl on defrost setting for 3-4 minutes. Stir and leave the mixture to stand before spooning over the pears.

Serving tip

Serve with small sponge-finger biscuits or wafers half coated with chocolate - an irresistible combination! To drink, a glass of Poire Williams liqueur would be perfect.

*H*OT LEMON SOUFFLES MAGNIFIQUE

NORTHERN FRANCE

Impressive to behold but easy to make, this dessert is flavoured with the tang of lemons and baked as individual servings. These light, fluffy soufflés make a splendid finish to any meal.

INGREDIENTS

(Serves 4)

- 2 lemons
- butter, for greasing
- icing sugar, for sprinkling
- 60g/2½oz plain flour
- 250ml/9fl oz milk
- 1 tbsp butter
- 75g/3oz caster sugar
- 4 eggs

TO DECORATE

- icing sugar, for dusting

INGREDIENTS TIP

Instead of lemons, you can use other citrus fruits such as oranges or limes to make the soufflé. Try to avoid oranges that you know to be very sweet, however, as these would spoil the intended sharp flavour of the dessert.

1 Wash the lemons and dry. Pare off a strip of rind and cut into thinner strips. Halve the lemons and squeeze the juice.

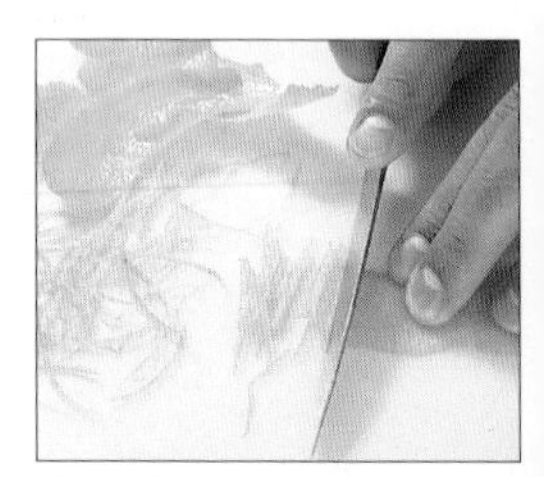

Step 1

2 Grease the base of four individual soufflé dishes (each with a capacity of about 175ml/6fl oz) with butter and sprinkle with the icing sugar. Preheat the oven to 190°C/375°F/Gas 5.

3 Mix the flour with 6 tablespoons milk, then gradually stir in the rest. Add the butter and half the caster sugar and transfer the mixture to a pan. Cook over a moderate heat for 1–2 minutes until the mixture thickens, whisking continuously to prevent lumps. Remove from the heat.

Step 3

4 Separate the eggs. Stir the egg yolks, lemon juice and rind into the soufflé mixture in the pan. Leave to cool.

5 Whisk the whites until stiff, then gradually whisk in the remaining sugar. Fold into the soufflé mixture, about one third at a time, then spoon into the dishes. Bake for 20 minutes, or until risen and golden in colour. Dust with sifted icing sugar and serve immediately.

Step 5

Preparation **25** Min Baking **20** Min

Per Serving: 263 kcal/1107 kJ;

10g protein; 10g fat; 36g carbohydrate

TYPICALLY FRENCH

Baked soufflés, both sweet and savoury, are very popular in France. They are ideal for the leisurely mealtimes the French enjoy. As soufflés collapse quickly after cooking, they are only made to order - guests must wait for their soufflé, never the other way around.

Cooking tip

Although the soufflés must be served as soon as they come out of the oven, you can prepare the mixture to the end of Step 4, up to 12 hours ahead. Dust the surface with a layer of extra caster sugar before cooling, to prevent a skin forming. Whisk and fold in the egg whites immediately before baking.

Serving tip

Serve the soufflés with mandarin orange segments – a pretty way is to arrange mandarins around the edge of four small plates and place the soufflés in the centre as soon as they are cooked.

PEACH MELBA

NORTHERN FRANCE

This famous dessert of lightly poached peaches is laced with a tangy fresh raspberry sauce. It was created for the celebrated Australian opera singer, Dame Nellie Melba.

INGREDIENTS

(Serves 4)

- 4 ripe peaches
- 100g/4oz granulated or caster sugar
- 600ml/1 pint water
- 2 tbsp lemon juice
- 225g/8oz raspberries
- 2-3 tbsp icing sugar
- 25g/1oz butter
- 25g/1oz flaked almonds
- 8 scoops vanilla ice cream and 8 wafers, to serve
- raspberries, to decorate

INGREDIENTS TIP

Choose fresh peaches that are ripe but still firm and free of any bruises or other blemishes. Frozen raspberries are perfectly good as a substitute for fresh. Thaw at room temperature for about 30 minutes before using.

1 Wipe or rinse the peaches and pat dry with kitchen paper. Put the granulated or caster sugar, water and lemon juice in a saucepan and heat gently until the sugar dissolves. Bring to the boil, then reduce the heat and simmer for 5 minutes.

2 Add the peaches and poach for 10 minutes, or until tender, turning them over once or twice during the cooking time. Lift from the syrup with a draining spoon and leave to cool on a plate.

3 Put the raspberries and icing sugar in a food processor and purée until smooth. Sieve to remove the seeds, if preferred. Chill for 1 hour or until ready to serve.

4 Melt the butter in a frying pan. Add the almonds and fry, gently stirring, until lightly browned. Tip onto a plate lined with kitchen paper and leave to cool.

5 Slit the skins of the peaches with a sharp knife and peel. Put each peach in a serving dish and add 2 scoops of vanilla ice cream and 2 wafers. Spoon over the raspberry sauce, sprinkle with the almonds. Decorate with raspberries and serve at once.

Step 2

Step 3

Step 4

Preparation **30** Min
Cooking **10** Min
Chilling **1** Hour
Per Serving: 379 kcal/1595 kJ
6g protein; 16g fat; 56g carbohydrate

TYPICALLY FRENCH

The great French chef Auguste Escoffier was famous for his culinary skills during the 1890s. He devised this dish in 1892 for Dame Nellie Melba who was singing at the Opera House. His tradition is carried on today by chefs across the country.

Cooking tip

Peaches are fragile when hot, so handle them as little as possible until they cool, to keep the skin intact and avoid damaging the fruit. Be particularly careful when moving the hot peaches from the pan. It is easier to peel a cool peach, and the cool fruit also keeps its shape better during handling, improving the appearance of the dish.

Serving tip

Peach Melba is a refreshing fruity dessert ideal for serving after a full-flavoured main course such as a spicy tomato and fish casserole.

SERVING TIP Serve with cappuccino: half a cup of delicious, strong espresso coffee topped up with frothy milk, and traditionally served sprinkled with cocoa powder or ground cinnamon.

ZABAGLIONE WITH RED BERRIES

NORTHERN ITALY

INGREDIENTS

(Serves 4)

- 1 small lemon
- 250g/9oz mixed red berries (redcurrants, strawberries, raspberries)
- 5 tbsp caster sugar
- 4 large egg yolks
- 4 tbsp Marsala

TO DECORATE

- lemon balm sprigs

INGREDIENTS TIP

Marsala, the fortified wine from Sicily, is the most famous Italian dessert wine and comes in different styles - use a sweet or dry one, whichever you prefer. You can substitute other dessert wines, or sherry or port.

This deliciously boozy dessert from the Piedmont region simply melts in the mouth. The light-as-air mixture is whisked with sweet Marsala wine until frothy.

1 Wash the lemon in hot water and dry. Grate the rind with a fine grater, then cut in half and squeeze the juice.

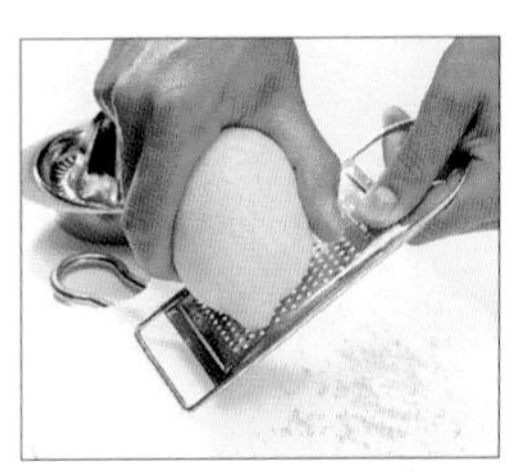

Step 1

2 Wash the berries. Pull the redcurrants very carefully from the stalks with the prongs of a fork. Pull the stalks from the strawberries. Keep a few small strawberries whole and halve or quarter any large ones.

3 Sprinkle the fruit with 1 tablespoon of the sugar and the lemon juice. Cover and chill for 1 hour.

Step 3

4 Just before serving, bring a little water to the boil in a saucepan and reduce to a simmer. Put the yolks, remaining sugar, lemon rind and Marsala in a small bowl and place it over the saucepan. Don't let the bowl touch the water. Beat vigorously with an electric whisk, or a balloon whisk, for about 5 minutes until the mixture becomes light and fluffy and doubles in volume.

Step 4

5 Quickly pour into four glasses and divide the fruit between them. (Some of the fruit will sink, the rest will sit on the top.) Decorate with lemon balm sprigs.

Preparation **30** Min Chilling **1** Hour
Per Serving: 128 kcal/532 kJ;
5g protein; 8g fat; 6g carbohydrate

TYPICALLY PIEDMONTESE

The Piedmontese, living in the Piedmont region of north-western Italy, are master confectioners and dessert-makers. Visitors to Turin will find pastry shops full of exquisite delicacies such as *gianduotti* - bitter chocolates filled with soft chocolate flavoured with hazelnuts.

3 WAYS WITH FRESH FRUIT SALAD

Fruit salads are popular the world over. The fruits used vary according to what is available and national preferences but all are equally colourful and refreshing.

Basic Sugar Syrup

This syrup can be made in larger quantities than needed and stored in the fridge for up to a week.

(SERVES 4)
- 100g/4oz caster or granulated sugar
- 100ml/3½fl oz water

1 Heat the sugar and water in a heavy-based pan over a low heat until the sugar has dissolved completely.

2 Bring to the boil, reduce the heat and simmer gently for about 1 minute until the syrup is clear.

Spiced Exotic Fruits

Preparation: **15** Min Chilling: **2** Hours

Thailand

- 1 quantity basic sugar syrup
- ½ tsp ground ginger
- ½ tsp ground cinnamon
- pinch of grated nutmeg
- ¼ fresh pineapple
- 1 papaya
- 175g/6oz lychees
- 1 small mango
- 2 slices watermelon

3 While the sugar syrup is still hot, stir in the ginger, cinnamon and nutmeg. Leave until cold.

4 Peel the pineapple and remove the core. Halve and peel the papaya and scoop out the seeds. Peel the lychees, halve and remove the stones. Peel the mango and cut the flesh away from the stone. Peel and deseed the watermelon.

5 Cut all the fruit, except the lychees, into bite-sized pieces. Place in a large glass bowl and pour over the syrup.

6 Chill for 2 hours. Remove from the fridge about 30 minutes before serving to return to room temperature.

Mint Fruit Salad

Preparation: **20** Min Chilling: **2–3** Hours

Great Britain

- 1 quantity basic sugar syrup
- 2 sprigs fresh mint
- 225g/8oz strawberries
- 1 large, ripe pear
- 2 bananas
- juice of 1 lemon
- 100g/4oz seedless green grapes

TO DECORATE

- a few fresh mint leaves

3 While the sugar syrup is still warm, add the mint sprigs and leave to cool. When cold, remove and discard the mint.

4 Remove the stalks from the strawberries and cut into quarters or halves. Quarter, core, peel and slice the pear. Peel and slice bananas.

5 In a large glass toss the pears and bananas in the lemon juice. Add the strawberries. Pull the grapes from the stalks and add to the bowl.

6 Pour the syrup over the fruit and chill for 2–3 hours. Remove from the fridge about 30 minutes before serving and decorate with the fresh mint.

Golden Orchard Fruits

Preparation: **20** Min

France

- 1 quantity sugar syrup made with dry white wine instead of water
- 100ml/3½fl oz muscat or other sweet dessert wine
- 2 peaches
- 225g/8oz apricots
- 2 nectarines
- 25g/1oz toasted flaked almonds

3 Allow the sugar syrup to cool and then stir in the sweet dessert wine.

4 Place the peaches in a heatproof bowl and pour over boiling water to cover. Leave to stand for 1 minute, drain and cool under cold water. Slit the skins and then peel them off.

5 Halve the peaches, apricots and nectarines. Remove the stones and cut the fruit into neat slices.

6 Put the fruit in a glass serving dish and pour over the syrup. Scatter over the toasted flaked almonds and serve.

SICILIAN STUFFED PEACHES

SOUTHERN ITALY

Juicy, sweet peaches are filled with crushed almond biscuits, soaked in Marsala dessert wine and briefly baked in the oven. Lightly dusted with icing sugar, they're a delicious treat.

INGREDIENTS
(Serves 4)

- 4 unskinned almonds
- 4 large peaches
- 3 tbsp butter
- 75g/3oz amaretti (almond biscuits)
- 100ml/3½fl oz dry Marsala or orange juice
- 1 tbsp lemon juice
- 1 egg yolk
- 2 tbsp caster sugar

TO DECORATE

- icing sugar, for dusting
- fresh mint sprigs

INGREDIENTS TIP

Amaretti are small Italian almond biscuits. If unavailable, you could use ratafias or macaroons. Almonds with their skins on are fresher and sweeter than ready-skinned ones.

1 Cover the almonds with boiling water for 2–3 minutes. Drain in a sieve, then slip them out of their skin.

2 Cover the peaches with boiling water for 1–2 minutes, drain, cool and peel off the skin. Cut in half and remove the stone. Spoon out some of the flesh from the cavity and put in a bowl. Mash with a fork.

3 Preheat the oven to 200°C/400°F/Gas 6. Grease a shallow ovenproof dish with 1 tablespoon of the butter.

4 Place amaretti biscuits in a polythene bag and crush to fine crumbs with a rolling pin. Sprinkle with 2–3 tablespoons of Marsala or orange juice and stir into the peach mash. Add the lemon juice, egg yolk and sugar and stir well. Spoon the mixture into the peach halves. Place the stuffed peaches in the greased dish, adding an almond to each.

5 Dice the remaining butter and put on top of the biscuit mixture. Pour the rest of the Marsala or orange juice over the peaches. Bake for 15 minutes, or until the topping is crisp. To serve, dust with sifted icing sugar and decorate with mint sprigs.

Step 1

Step 2

Step 4

Preparation **35** Min Cooking **15** Min
Per Serving: 342 kcal/1427 kJ;
5g protein; 21g fat;
27g carbohydrate

TYPICALLY SICILIAN

The people of Sicily – the volcanic island set in the Mediterranean sea at the toe of Italy – are renowned for their sweet tooth. Stuffed peaches, known locally as *pesche ripiene*, is a particular favourite. Another Sicilian speciality is the ice-cream cake *cassata*.

Cooking tip

Removing the peach skin is not absolutely necessary, but it improves the texture of the finished dessert. If you prefer, use nectarines, which do not need peeling • The peach stones could be cracked and the kernels used for decoration.

Serving tip

The sweet fruitiness of stuffed peaches makes a tasty dessert following a main course of roast chicken or lamb. The perfect accompaniment to the stuffed peaches is a glass of Marsala.

CHERRY CLAFOUTIS

SOUTHERN FRANCE

Evoking the spirit of rural France, this is a spectacular and delicious dessert. Sweet cherries are baked in a crisp, golden batter and dusted with icing sugar.

INGREDIENTS

(Serves 4)

- 500g/1lb 2oz sweet cherries
- butter, for greasing
- 3 eggs
- 2 tbsp icing sugar
- pinch of salt
- 4 tbsp plain flour
- 200ml/7fl oz milk

TO DECORATE

- icing sugar, for dusting

INGREDIENTS TIP

In France, this dish would be made with a mixture of sweet and sour cherries, such as Morello. Sour cherries are too bitter to eat raw but taste excellent cooked. They are rarely available fresh in Great Britain, but they can be bought canned or bottled and used in this recipe.

1 Wash the cherries and dry on kitchen paper. Reserve a few with stalks for decoration. Remove the stone from the remaining cherries with a cherry stoner to keep the fruit whole.

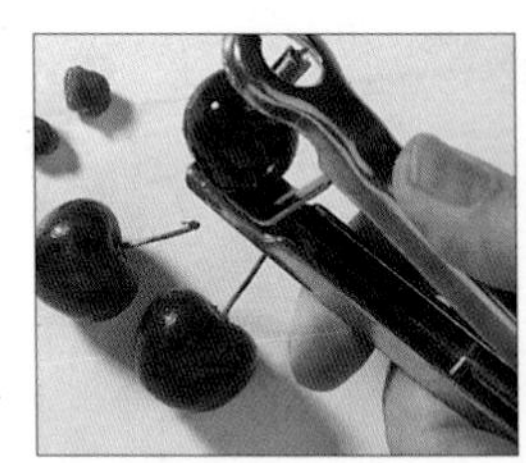

Step 1

2 Preheat the oven to 170°C/325°F/Gas 3. Grease a shallow 25cm/10in diameter ovenproof dish with butter.

3 Combine the eggs with the icing sugar and salt, and whisk until light and frothy. Stir in the flour 1 tablespoon at a time, adding 2 tablespoons milk with each addition of flour. Stir in the rest of the milk.

Step 3

4 Spread the stoned cherries evenly over the base of the greased dish and spoon the batter over the top.

Step 4

5 Bake for 35 minutes, or until the batter is set and lightly browned. If the cherries start to brown, cover the dish with foil until the batter is set.

6 Leave to cool a little, then dust the top with sifted icing sugar. Decorate with the reserved cherries and serve warm.

Preparation **25** Min Cooking **35** Min
Per Serving: 175 kcal/739 kJ;
8g protein; 5g fat; 26g carbohydrate

TYPICALLY FRENCH

Cherries are grown all over France, and are particularly popular in the Limousin region – the French know this dish as clafoutis limousin. As well as being an ingredient of sweet dishes, cherries also make a sharp sauce, used to accompany rich meats such as duck or game.

Cooking tips

If using canned or bottled cherries in syrup drain well and reduce the amount of icing sugar to 1 teaspoon to compensate for the sweetness of the syrup • Fold the flour and milk into the egg mixture very lightly using a figure of eight movement. Over-mixing will make the dessert heavy and stodgy.

Serving tip

Serve with vanilla sauce: whisk 125ml/4fl oz milk, 4 tbsp caster sugar and 1 tbsp cornflour in a saucepan until smooth. Add 300ml/½ pint milk and cook gently until thickened. Stir in 1 tsp vanilla essence.

DICTIONARY OF TERMS

Fresh fruit is widely available all year round. Mix with spices and aromatic flavourings or top with cream or yoghurt for truly tempting desserts.

CREAM AND YOGHURT

The classic topping for a fruit dessert is a swirl of whipped cream. Cream is a frequent ingredient as well. Yoghurt adds a similar texture and a sharper flavour than cream but the two are not always interchangeable.

CREAM

Types of cream are defined by their fat content:
Double cream *contains about 50% fat and* ***whipping cream*** *35–40%. Both are easy to whip to soft peaks and hold their shape for several hours. The best cream for heating is double – it becomes deliciously syrupy so is ideal for custards and sweet sauces. Whipping can be added to hot dishes but separates if boiled. Creams with less than 35% fat (such as* ***single*** *and* ***half-fat****) become granular and won't thicken if whipped — the same also happens to over-whipped double or whipping cream.* ***Single cream*** *has about 18% fat; it is perfect for pouring over a dessert but will not whip and curdles if boiled. If you do want to boil single cream, stir in 1 teaspoon cornflour to each 150ml/¼ pint cream beforehand.*

Crème fraîche *is the standard in France. It contains up to 60% fat, but is available in low-fat versions (again these separate if boiled). It is thicker than other creams and tastes slightly sour or sharp, which prevents a sweet dessert becoming too cloying.*

YOGHURT

Yoghurt is a fermented milk product, increasingly used in low-fat sweet desserts. It cannot be whipped and separates when boiled, but can be heated to just below boiling point in hot dessert sauces. To thicken yoghurt add cornflour (which stabilizes it) as for single cream.
Very low-fat yoghurt *is made from skimmed milk. It can be used in place of single cream for topping sweet desserts.*
Natural yoghurt *contains no artificial additives; 'bio' varieties contain natural bacteria, which may promote good health. It is available in various thicknesses.*
Greek-style yoghurt *is thick and creamy. Stir in surface liquid to thin the yoghurt or pour it off for a thicker consistency. Stir into sauces, add to dips or spoon over fruit.*

Alcoholic drinks, including spirits, liqueurs and fortified wines, are often added to desserts to give a distinctive richness. When boiled, alcohol evaporates but not when simply heated or stirred into a cold dish. Take care not to add too much or serve the dish to children or anyone who prefers not to drink alcohol.

Caramel is made by heating sugar – the liquid from the dissolved sugar evaporates and a golden brown syrup is formed. It becomes crisp and brittle once it has cooled.

Cobbler is a baked fruit pudding covered with a layer of golden sponge topping (in the American style), or overlapping rounds of scone dough (in the British way).

Coconut is used in many exotic fruit desserts. Coconut is rich in vitamins, protein and natural oils but high in saturated fat. Fresh coconut milk from the centre of the coconut is watery and greyish. At the supermarket you can buy canned coconut milk or coconut cream in small cartons. Both are white, unsweetened and have the consistency of single cream. Creamed coconut comes in a block and is sold in packets. It is solid and must be cut with a knife or grated. Desiccated coconut is finely grated dried coconut. Either sweetened or unsweetened, it is perfect for mixing with fruit or toasting as a topping.

Egg Yolks thicken and add richness to many sweet sauces, soufflés and mousses; the whisked whites add lightness and volume. Raw egg yolks should not be eaten by infants, pregnant women, the elderly or anyone in poor health.

Melon has many varieties. Galia is round with skin that turns from green to brown when ripe and succulent green flesh. Honeydew has white or yellow ridged skin, and pale flesh stronger on refreshment than flavour. Ogen is round with green skin and flesh, delicious in taste. Look out for Charentais, with its pale green skin and fragrant orange flesh, ideal for sorbets. If storing melons in the fridge, wrap them up well or other food will smell melony.

Segmenting Fruit, such as orange and grapefruit, is necessary for many dessert recipes. Cut away the skin by slicing across the top of the fruit, then cut in a spiral around it. Cut as close to the flesh as possible. Remove any remaining white pith. Cut into the centre of the fruit along the membranes, so that each whole segment lifts out cleanly. Work over a plate to catch the juice. A sharp serrated knife is the best implement; always cut away from the hand that is holding the fruit.

Setting Agents, such as gelatine, are used to set fruit desserts. The most common is of animal origin, sold powdered in sachets, but supermarkets stock a vegetarian substitute. Always follow the packet instructions.

Zester or Canelle Knife is used for removing the rind from citrus fruits in very fine, matchstick strips, leaving the bitter pith behind. It curls the rind slightly as it peels it off, making an attractive decoration for mousses and cheesecakes.

Spices and Aromatic Flavourings

Add a spice to a dessert and it becomes a gift from the east – these are some of the best to use with exotic fruit.

Allspice

Generally sold ground, its flavour is a mixture of cinnamon, cloves and nutmeg, which is how it got its name. Particularly associated with fruit pies.

Cinnamon

This spice has a sweet, 'warm' flavour. Available as rolled sticks (it is actually a bark) or ground. Cinnamon sugar is delicious sprinkled over hot fruit fritters and puddings.

Ginger

Root ginger is sold fresh (to be peeled and sliced or grated), ground or preserved in syrup. It is traditionally served with melon.

Nutmeg

The aromatic seed of the tree, it is sold whole (for grating) or ground. Particularly associated with milk puddings.

Rose water

Distilled from rose petals or made from rose oil and water, it is used to flavour oriental desserts. Available at chemists.

Star anise

The dried, star-shaped fruit of a Chinese ever-green tree. Used whole or ground, it has an aniseed aroma and flavour.

Vanilla

Used in desserts as pods, extract or essence for its sweetish, mellow aroma.

INDEX

Acknowledgements

Picture Credits

All cover and recipe pictures:
Meister Verlag/International Masters Publisher B.V.
Karl Adamson, Michael Brauner, Dorothee Gödert, Neil Mersh
Agency pictures: *Introduction* Karl Adamson, Robert Harding
Pictures for the 'Typically' Sections Anthony Blake: page 20, 34, 52;
Bavaria: Benelux Press, page 9; PP, page 16; Wisniewski, page 42;
Reinhard, page 46; Higuchi, page 39; Bilder Pur: Uselmann, page 44
Colorific: page 36; IFA: Romann, page 6
Image Bank: Castaneda, page 12;
Helga Lade: Bramaz, page 26; Siwik, page 40; Lowes, page 50;
Pictures, page 57
Schapowalow: Reichelt, page 24; Loos, page 29, 30;
Pratt-Pries, page 32, 60; Atlantide, page 58
Silvestris: Pani/ Jeske, page 10; Prato, page 14
Tony Stone: Randkley, page 19; Camille, page 48

Measuring Ingredients
Tsp = teaspoon, Tbsp = tablespoon
Teaspoons and tablespoons are level and measured using standard measuring spoons.
Follow either metric or imperial measurements; don't mix the two.

© International Masters Publishers BV

International Masters Publishers Ltd MCMXCVIII
Reproduced by Studio One Origination, London, UK
Printed in Verona, Italy, by Druck Mondadori

All rights reserved. No part of this book may be reproduced or transmitted in any form or by any means, electronic or mechanical, including translating, photocopying, recording or by any information storage and retrieval system without permission in writing from the publisher.